Genre Realis

MW01104825

Essential Ques...
How can others inspire us?

A Speech to Remember

by **Catriona Browne** • illustrated by **Theo Bain**

I am giving a speech at school today. I've written my speech, and I practiced it at home. Now I am waiting at the side of the stage. My legs feel heavy. My stomach is in knots, and I want to run away.

The One Voice singers are on first. Four of the singers are huddled together. They are **extremely** excited. The fifth singer, Della, stands by herself. She looks very **calm**.

I want to ask Della how she stays so calm. I notice that she is taking slow, deep breaths.

"Are you scared?" I ask.

"A little," Della says. "But not as scared as when I tried out for One Voice. I opened my mouth, and a **weird** squeak came out. I had cotton mouth."

"What's cotton mouth?" I ask.

"It's when your mouth is so dry it feels like it is full of cotton balls," Della says.

"What did you do?" I ask.

"I took a sip of water. Then I took some deep breaths," Della says. "Each time I breathed out, I got rid of some of my **fear**."

"Did it work?" I ask.

"Yes, I won a place in the group," Della says. "Before I go onstage now, I breathe my fears out."

"I'll try that," I say.

STOP AND CHECK

How does Della stay calm?

5

It's time for One Voice to go onstage. Della starts singing on her own. She opens her mouth … but instead of words, she just sings the notes. The others in the group look at each other with wide eyes. Della has forgotten the words!

Then Della starts to sing.

"*We try our best...*"

She **pauses** for a moment. Then she starts again.

"*We try our best to remember the words,*
But sometimes the words come out wrong.
We try our best to get it just right,
But sometimes we mess up the song!
Don't stop, just breathe, and keep singing."

The group joins with Della's new words.

As Della comes off the stage, I give her a high five.

"I forgot the words and had to make some up," she says.

"Everyone liked it!" I say.

"I was on a roller coaster. I couldn't get off, but I thought I might as well enjoy the ride," says Della.

Then I hear my name, Marnie Riley, being called.

"Break a leg," says Della. I know she says that to wish me luck. But it almost comes true. I trip and nearly fall over a cord. The pages of my speech fly all around. I get a little **flustered**. I gather up the pages and hurry onto the stage.

STOP AND CHECK

Why does Della tell Marnie to break a leg?

Chapter 3 The Speech

I'm standing on the stage. Everyone is staring at me. My face is hot. My mouth is dry. It's hard to read the first page.

I look to the side of the stage. Della is waving something.

I take a deep breath. As I breathe out, I look at the pages. I can see the words now, so I begin.

The speech goes well. It's like the **comment** Della made about the roller coaster. We are on a ride, the audience and me.

My speech builds up to the end. It's like the **steepest** climb of the roller coaster. Then, just when we reach the top of the ride, I come to a stop. The last page of my speech is missing!

STOP AND CHECK

What happened to the last page of Marnie's speech?

I'm not afraid. I know the car will stay on the track. I know how the speech should end. But I decide to do something different. I feel **adventurous** and almost **courageous**. I decide to talk about fear.

"This speech is about things that inspire me. Did you know that the word 'inspire' means to breathe in. I was afraid to give this speech, but someone taught me to breathe in and out slowly. She showed me how to keep going. She inspired me."

I look at Della. I begin to **recite** aloud:

"We try our best to remember the words,
But sometimes the words come
out wrong..."

Then Della and her group walk onto the stage and start singing.

"We try our best to get it just right,
But sometimes we mess up the song!
Don't stop, just breathe, and keep singing.
Don't stop, just breathe, and keep singing."

I join in. The audience claps. And that is the end of my speech.

STOP AND CHECK

Why does Marnie start saying Della's song?

Respond to Reading

Summarize

Summarize *A Speech to Remember.* Use details from the text. The chart may help you.

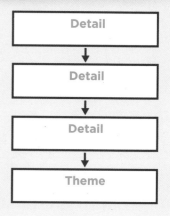

Text Evidence

1. How does Della inspire Marnie? Look at page 14 for clues. Theme

2. Find the word *trip* on page 9. What does it mean? What clues help you figure it out? Vocabulary

3. Write about the details the author uses to describe how Marnie feels during the story. Write About Reading

Compare Texts
Read about an inspiring singer-songwriter.

Let the Lion Roar

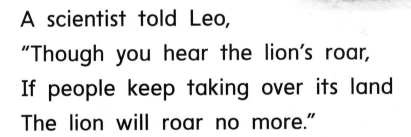

Leo played folk tunes.
Leo sang songs.
When Leo went to Africa,
He heard a lion roar.

A scientist told Leo,
"Though you hear the lion's roar,
If people keep taking over its land
The lion will roar no more."

He said, "People chase the lion
From its home on the warm savannah.
The fields become farms and factories.
Soon the lion will roar no more."

Leo wrote a folk tune,
Leo sang a song,
A song to save the lions
Titled *Let the Lion Roar.*

Leo toured the country.
Leo topped the charts.
Leo and his folk tune,
Let the Lion Roar.

People heard the message;
They began to change their ways.
They organized a movement
Called "Let the Lion Roar."

They said, "Don't tear up the planet,
Do not harm the land.
This world's not just for humans;
Please, let the lion roar."

People gave money.
People changed laws.
People sang with one voice,
"Let the Lion Roar."

Today the planet holds its breath—
Did the changes come too late?
Meanwhile in Africa, for now,
You still hear the lions roar.

 Make Connections

Can you think of a song that has inspired you the way Leo's song inspired people in *Let the Lion Roar*?

Essential Question

In what way is Della in *A Speech to Remember* like Leo in *Let the Lion Roar*? Text to Text

Focus on
Literary Elements

Repetition Poetry is language that has rhythms and patterns. The patterns are made by repeating sounds and rhymes. When rhymes and rhythms repeat, it is called repetition.

Read and Find The poem *Let the Lion Roar* has a rhythm that repeats. Repetition of the words helps to give a strong rhythm. Read the poem aloud to hear the rhythm clearly.

Your Turn

Work with a partner. Reread *Let the Lion Roar.* What words does the poet repeat? Why do you think the poet used repetition?